SUSTAINING UNCONVENTIONAL WARFARE

ABSTRACT

SUSTAINING UNCONVENTIONAL WARFARE, by MAJ John W. McGrady, 46 pages.

U.S. Special Operations Command (SOCOM) has publicly acknowledged that special operations forces (SOF) require conventional force support. Sustainment is a major component of that required conventional support. Review of the 2009 force design update (FDU) for the Band V Special Forces Group (SFG) shows that Special Forces (SF) operations in Iraq and Afghanistan, as well as the structure of the modular Brigade Combat Team (BCT) influenced the development of the SF Group Support Battalion (GSB) and the SF forward support companies (FSCs). As SF's primary mission, Unconventional Warfare should provide a central, unique, and specific influence in both organizational design and doctrine for all units within the SFG. However, the post-transformation Army's past decade of operations in the contemporary operating environment has influenced the design of the GSB and FSC in ways that do not optimize them for support of SF units conducting UW. One can easily see this influence when comparing the current SF sustainment structure with that of support units involved in the many historical examples of operations that fit the contemporary definition of unconventional warfare.

Three case studies analyzing historical UW operations in France and Greece illustrate common themes in UW sustainment. These themes highlight the shortcomings of the GSB and FSC construct in the Band V FDU by contrasting common characteristics of these organizations with the sustainment units that took part in the historical cases. Each case study bears adequate similarity to UW in the modern context according to the contemporary definition of UW to offer valuable insight. Sustainment operations and organizations are evaluated for economy, integration, and simplicity, three of the Army's principals of sustainment. The evaluation results in recommendations for the GSB and FSC that include limiting expansion of the GSB's common user land transportation (CULT) fleet, increased capability within the support operations (SPO) section, and the capability to coordinate for sustainment support from multiple levels of sustainment providers.

ACKNOWLEDGMENTS

I would like to thank first my monograph director, Dr. Mark Calhoun for his guidance during this research project. I enjoyed the freedom to both research and write what I learned throughout the process and as a result I have grown as a student of military art and science. I next thank COL James Sisemore, my seminar leader, for not only facilitating the opportunity to complete this research project, but also for establishing the professional environment throughout the course of the Advanced Military Studies Program necessary to develop students of military art and science. I also want to thank the staff at the Combined Arms Research Library, especially Michael Browne. I thoroughly enjoyed researching this monograph because of the environment they fostered and their assistance. Finally, I would like to thank my AMSP classmates. They are truly a crowd of honorable men and women, pressing up the hill of science with noble emulation.

TABLE OF CONTENTS

ACRONYMS

AEF	Allied Expeditionary Forces
ARSOF	Army Special Operations Forces
BCT	Brigade Combat Team
BLO	British Liaison Officer
BMM	British Military Mission
CJSOTF	Combined Joint Special Operations Task Force
CNT	Counter Narcotics and Terrorism
COE	Contemporary Operating Environment
COI	Coordinator for Information
EAM	Greek National Front
ELAS	Greek People's Liberation Army
ESC	Expeditionary Sustainment Command
FID	Foreign Internal Defense
FDU	Force Design Update
FSC	Forward Support Company
GDA	Greek Democratic Army
GSB	Group Support Battalion
JCET	Joint Combined Exchange Training
JOE	Joint Operating Environment
KKE	Greek Communist Party
NOF	Macedonian National Liberation Front
OEF	Operation ENDURING FREEDOM
OIF	Operation IRAQI FREEDOM
OSS	Office of Strategic Services
SA/G	Special Activities/Goodfellow
SB	Sustainment Brigade

SF	Special Forces
SFG	Special Forces Group
SIS	British Secret Intelligence Service
SO	Special Operations Branch of the OSS
SOCOM	Special Operations Command
SOE	Special Operations Executive
SOF	Special Operations Forces
SOTF	Special Operations Task Force
TSOC	Theater Special Operations Command
TOE	Table of Organization and Equipment
USASFC(A)	United States Army Special Forces Command (Airborne)
UW	Unconventional Warfare

ILLUSTRATION

INTRODUCTION

> ...in time of war... it became a natural thing for anyone who wanted a change of government to call in help from the outside.
> –Thucydides, *History of the Peloponnesian War*

> ...it was not a shortage of supplies which held up the largest possible force, but it was the delivery of those supplies at the right time and place.
> –Major General Sir Colin Gubbins, lecture to the Joint Royal United Services Institute, 28 January, 1948

BACKGROUND

U.S. Special Operations Command (SOCOM) has publicly acknowledged that special operations forces (SOF) require conventional force support. Sustainment is a major component of that required conventional support. The SOCOM Commander stated in 2012 that SOCOM would not attempt to "grow organic 'enablers' that duplicate Service-provided capabilities at the same rate as our operational elements."[1] However, the U.S. Army Special Forces Command (Airborne) (USASFC(A)) is in the midst of transforming its sustainment force structure to something very similar to conventional force sustainment structure.

Review of the 2009 force design update (FDU) for the Band V Special Forces Group (SFG) shows that Special Forces (SF) operations in Iraq and Afghanistan, as well as the structure of the modular Brigade Combat Team (BCT) influenced the development of the SF Group Support Battalion (GSB) and the SF forward support companies (FSCs).[2] USASFC(A) assessed that there was a need for "organic sustainment capability for prolonged operations in under-developed global areas."[3] The ratio of dwell time (the amount of time spent at home station

---

[1] William H. McRaven, "Posture Statement of Admiral William H. McRaven, USN, Commander, United States Special Operations Command," (2012).

[2] Each Band within a FDU represents an iteration in the SFG's transformation. The first four Bands added an SF Battalion and GSB to each SFG. The Band V FDU established FSCs similar to conventional force FSCs.

[3] United States Army Special Forces Command (Airborne), "Operational and Organization Concept Paper for USASFC(A) Changes to the SF Group(A)," (Accessed 14

1

between deployments) to deployment time for USASFC(A) personnel fell to 1:0.87, meaning

nearly all SF Battalions spent as much time deployed as they did at home station. The

contemporary table of organization and equipment (TOE) proved insufficient to meet the

requirements of such numerous combat deployments.[4] While reduced operations in Iraq have

changed the requirements for SF, the operational environment remains in such a state that,

according to the 2010 "Joint Operating Environment" (JOE) document, it "will keep Special

Forces busy."[5] In addition to the contemporary operating environment (COE), the ongoing

transformation of the sustainment structure within the conventional army affected the design of

the GSB and FSC.

Figure 1 below illustrates the effect Army Transformation had on the design of the SFG

sustainment organization.[6]

September 2012), https://ako.us.army.mil/suite/designer, 2. This document was held in the Army's Force Design Directorate's shared files on Army Knowledge Online, but is no longer available.

[4]Ibid.; United States Army Special Forces Command (Airborne), "Organization Design Paper for USASFC(A) Changes to the Special Forces Group(A)," (Accessed 14 September 2012), https://ako.us.army.mil/suite/designer, 3. For every 100 days in dwell, a Soldier assigned to USASFC(A) would serve 87 days deployed. This document was also held in the Army's Force Design Directorate's shared files on Army Knowledge Online, but is no longer available.

[5]United States Joint Forces Command, "The Joint Operating Environment 2010," (Accessed 14 September 2012), www.jfcom.mil/newslink/storyarchive/2010/JOE_2010_o.pdf, 68.

[6]U.S. Army, Field Manual 3-05.140, *Army Special Operations Forces Logistics*, (Washington, D.C.: Government Printing Office, 2009), 2-3.

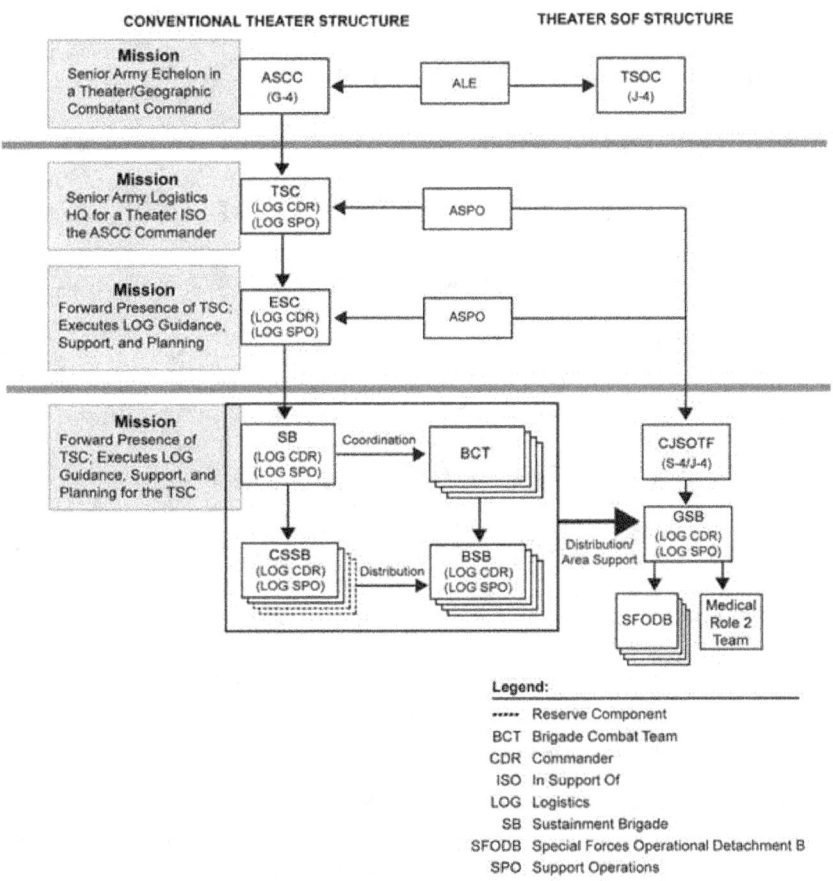

CONVENTIONAL THEATER STRUCTURE   THEATER SOF STRUCTURE

Legend:

- - - - Reserve Component
BCT   Brigade Combat Team
CDR   Commander
ISO   In Support Of
LOG   Logistics
SB   Sustainment Brigade
SFODB   Special Forces Operational Detachment B
SPO   Support Operations

Figure 1. Typical ARSOF Sustainment Structure.

The figure shows relationships between sustainment organizations in a combat theater, but it

implies both that SF will operate in a theater with robust sustainment architecture and that the SF

sustainment organization corresponds to a conventional sustainment organization. In other words,

Figure 1 depicts modular conventional force organizations, such as a sustainment brigade (SB), in

such a way that it makes it seem like they operate in the same manner as an SFG.[7] The figure fails

to depict clearly the fact that the combined joint special operations task force (CJSOTF) may

operate throughout the same geographical area as the expeditionary sustainment command (ESC).

A CJSOTF, commanded by a colonel, could be responsible for special operations within the same

---

[7]SFGs typically serve as a combined joint special operations task force (CJSOTF)
subordinate to a theater special operations command (TSOC).

3

area that an ESC, commanded by a major general is responsible for sustainment operations. It also does not illustrate the scalable nature of SF units and their missions. An SF mission can be as large as a CJSOTF, or as small as the three-man detachment.

During Operations IRAQI FREEDOM and ENDURING FREEDOM (OIF and OEF, respectively) one CJSOTF operated throughout the same geographical space as one ESC and multiple SBs. CJSOTFs in both theaters coordinated directly with the theater special operations command (TSOC) sustainment staff section (J-4) and ESCs for sustainment support. The GSBs supported both large-scale operations, such as OIF and OEF, as well as smaller missions. Joint combined exchange training (JCET) exercises, counter narcotic and terrorist (CNT) operations and pre-mission training all required GSB sustainment support. Figure 1 does not address the sustainment structure for these physically smaller, but no less operationally important, missions. While often small in size and duration, these are often the most significant missions that SF performs.

Sustaining Unconventional Warfare

The Army designed SF specifically for unconventional warfare, defined in JP 3-05 as "activities conducted to enable a resistance movement or insurgency to coerce, disrupt, or overthrow a government or occupying power by operating through or with an underground, auxiliary, and guerrilla force in a denied area."[8] While many organizations within the Department of Defense (DOD) can perform operations similar to or in support of UW, only SF possesses the specific characteristics intended to optimize it for UW. JP 3-05 defines additional SOF core that include direct action (DA), counterterrorism (CT), information operations (IO), military information support operations (MISO) as well as civil affairs (CA). SOCOM provides these

---

[8]Department of Defense, Joint Publication 3-05, *Special Operations*, (Washington, D.C.: Government Printing Office, 2011), GL-13-14; U.S. Army, Field Manual 3-18, *Special Forces Operations*, (Washington, D.C.: Government Printing Office, 2012), 2-5.

capabilities within its different units, and SF uniquely provides UW.[9] This unique requirement results in several aspects of SF that provide a better understanding of SF units' organizational design. First, all SF missions are based on UW in fact, as stated in FM 3-18, Special Forces Operations, UW provides "the methods and skill sets by which all other Special Forces missions are accomplished."[10] Further, the scalability of a UW campaign is drastically different in size and function than a conventional land campaign. Finally, UW is a distinct form of war requiring a distinct form of sustainment. Given these three aspects of UW, the UW mission set should dominate all other influences in the organizational design of the sustainment organizations within the SFG.

The Army derives all SF missions from their UW capabilities. Given their ability to enter a country and provide both materiel and training for a military force, they offer an easily transferable capability set. The foreign internal defense (FID) mission illustrates this characteristic.[11] Both FID and UW involve U.S. forces supporting a foreign military organization, but in addition to these common characteristics the two missions have several major differences. FID operations consist of support to an existing government, while UW operations consist of support to an indigenous forces' attempt to coerce, disrupt, or overthrow an existing government. FID provides a host nation's military organization with the ability to cope with internal threats. By contrast, UW assists a group in developing the military capability that is an internal threat to the government it seeks to coerce or overthrow.[12] Finally, a unit as small as a single 12-man

---

[9]Multiple SOCOM units can provide direct action or counterterrorism capabilities, but some are unique to organizations, such as CA and MISO.

[10]FM 3-18, 2-4.

[11]JP 3-05, GL-7. JP 3-05 defines FID as participation by civilian and military agencies of a government in any of the action programs taken by another governmnet or other designated organization to free and protect its society from subversion, lawlessness, insurgency, terrorism, and other threats to its security.

[12]FM 3-18, 2-8.

operational detachment – alpha (ODA) can conduct FID, which illustrates the second unique aspect of UW: its scalability.

The size of units conducting a UW campaign can cover a broad spectrum. History provides many examples of UW operations taking place in conjunction with conventional combat operations. Some large-scale examples include the operations conducted by the U.S. Office of Strategic Services (OSS) in Europe, the Mediterranean, and Asia during the Second World War; the Soviet partisan movement in Eastern Europe during the same conflict; and the SF involvement in Operation IRAQI FREEDOM. However, many examples of much smaller UW campaigns exist including the U.S. support to operations in Afghanistan during the 1980s, the U.S. in North Vietnam in the early 1960s, and those of several Eastern European countries in Greece from 1946-1949.[13] One common factor exists in these otherwise very different examples – each involved a sustainment organization that possessed the same flexibility and scalability as the unit conducting UW operations. This flexibility and scalability required a unique type of military organization, which in turn required a unique type of sustainment.

U.S. Army Training Circular 18-01, *Special Forces Unconventional Warfare*, (TC 18-01) advises UW practitioners to rely on "confiscation, barters or trades, IOUs, donations or levies" to meet their tactical supply requirements in an unconventional warfare operational area (UWOA).[14] These methods differ drastically from conventional U.S. Army units' tactical sustainment methods. Further, UW campaigns require two distinct concepts of support for two organizations conducting the campaign: the guerrilla, or resistance, force and the SF force. This naturally leads to a departure from conventional concepts of support. FM 3-18 also highlights three concerns specific to UW: reduced numbers of sustainment personnel due to the time required to train them,

---

[13]U.S. Army, Training Circular 18-01, *Special Forces Unconventional Warfare*, (Washington, D.C.: Government Printing Office, 2011), 8.

[14]Ibid., 3-9.

the need to conduct sustainment operations under covert or clandestine conditions, and the need

for SF personnel to perform functions normally provided by sustainment personnel.[15] Given this

disparity, *TC 18-01* provides a doctrinal explanation of how SF units sustain UW: outside of the

UWOA a special operations task force (SOTF) performs the necessary sustainment functions to

support both ODAs and guerrilla forces.[16] Service detachments and GSBs enable SF battalions

and groups to perform these sustainment tasks as a SOTF (under the Band V FDU, the FSC will

replace the service detachment).

As SF's primary mission, UW should provide a central, unique, and specific influence in

both organizational design and doctrine for all units within the SFG. However, the post-

transformation Army's past decade of operations in the COE has influenced the design of the

GSB and FSC in ways that do not optimize them for support of SF units conducting UW. One can

easily see this influence when comparing the current SF sustainment structure with that of support

units involved in the many historical examples of operations that fit the contemporary definition

of unconventional warfare. In the words of historian John Lewis Gaddis, historical study gives the

opportunity to "interpret the past for the purposes of the present with a view to managing the

future."[17] With this idea as a guiding principle, one can use historical examples to identify flaws

in the current U.S. Army SF sustainment structure and identify potential solutions.

Methodology

SF organizations conduct two basic categories of missions: unconventional warfare (UW)

and foreign internal defense (FID).[18] While related, the two missions differ significantly. Despite

---

[15]FM 3-18.

[16]TC 18-01, 3-11.

[17]John Lewis Gaddis, *The Landscape of History: How Historians Map the Past* (Oxford, N.Y.: Oxford University Press, 2002).

[18]FM 3-18, xv.

this fact, when Army planners redesigned the GSB and FSC, they did not account for the dominant influence of UW as an SF mission. Further, USASFC(A) assumed in 2009 that the most likely group and battalion level deployments would "entail bare based austere indigenous support conditions."[19] While this seemed a valid prediction in the initial phases of both OEF and OIF, each mission eventually resembled FID as opposed to UW.[20]

The U.S. Army Special Operations Command (USASOC) is currently in the process of modernizing the organizational design of its sustainment units. It must provide those units with a very specific capability set to optimize their ability to perform their intended combat role. The USASOC planners modernizing the organizational design of these sustainment units must take into account the unique mission requirements of their supported units. Specifically, in accordance with SF doctrine, SFG support units must possess the capability to support operational units performing the critical and unique UW mission. However, contemporary SF operations in Iraq and Afghanistan, as well as the force structure of the post-Transformation modular brigade combat team (BCT) and its associated sustainment organizational design have significantly influenced the reorganization of the SFG's GSB and FSC. This has led to a shift in sustainment capabilities and organization based on specific lessons learned from specific conflicts, as opposed to the core capabilities and organization the Army requires the SFG to possess. The following analysis demonstrates the sub-optimal nature of these organizational structures for the conduct of UW by reviewing three historical cases to illustrate the organizational characteristics that made sustainment organization successful in these diverse UW campaigns. This supports recommendations for an adjustment in future U.S. Army SF sustainment organizations and

---

[19]United States Army Special Forces Command (Airborne), "Organization Design Paper for USASFC(A) Changes to the Special Forces Group(A)," 8.

[20]United States Special Operations Command, "USSOCOM History," http://www.fas.org/irp/agency/dod/socom/index.html. A summary of both UW campaigns can be found in pages 91-107 for OEF and 121 for OIF.

capabilities to optimize them better suited to the unique mission of UW, rather than the kinds of operations that they have supported over the past decade, which do not serve as useful generalized examples of UW operations.

Three case studies analyzing historical UW operations, one in France and two in Greece, illustrate common themes in UW sustainment. These themes highlight the shortcomings of the GSB and FSC construct in the Band V FDU by contrasting common characteristics of these organizations with the sustainment units that took part in the historical cases. Each case study bears adequate similarity to UW in the modern context according to the contemporary definition of UW to offer valuable insight. For example, each historical case involves an organization conducting UW after either recently forming or undergoing a significant transformation. In addition to their organizational similarity, the organizations involved in each case study conducted UW campaigns in a fashion similar to that seen in U.S. Army doctrine. In particular, each case involves a resistance movement, the use of force to achieve political goals, operations in a denied area and support from an external source.

During the French underground movement in the Second World War, both Britain and America waged a successful UW campaign – and the success of these campaigns relied heavily on the considerable sustainment support that each country provided to the French resistance and the units that supported it. In Greece from 1941 to 1949, two UW campaigns occurred. Britain ran the first against the German occupation forces, which ended in 1944. The second UW campaign, run by Yugoslavia, Albania, and Bulgaria, was a failed attempt to establish a communist state in Greece.

The U.S. Army's principles of sustainment (integration, anticipation, responsiveness, simplicity, economy, survivability, continuity, and improvisation) serve as a set of common evaluation criteria to assess each case according to a common set of measures.[21] The source of

---

[21]U.S. Army, Army Doctrine Publication 4-0, *Sustainment* (Washington, D.C.:

these criteria, *Army Doctrine Publication 4-0, Sustainment* (*ADP 4-0*) also states that the sustainment warfighting function "consists of three major elements: logistics, personnel services, and health service support."[22] This study will focus on logistics and personnel services. Assessment of the principles of sustainment related to health service support exceeds the scope of this study.

CASE STUDIES

France

Britain began to prepare for unconventional war against Germany long before German acts of aggression in 1939. In fact, the British Secret Intelligence Service (SIS) began research alternative methods of warfare against the Germans in the summer of 1935. They concluded that the only way to respond to UW attacks from the Germans was to employ the same methods. In January 1938, the British Army seconded MAJ Laurence Grand to the SIS to research sabotage. Shortly thereafter, in June, the British War Office assigned MAJ J. C. F. Holland to the General Staff (Research) (GS(R)) office with very little direction. He eventually built a small office that researched guerrilla warfare and produced British doctrine for aspects of UW.[23] By the end of the year, Britain had two organizations devoted to research and conduct of UW, a desirable capability in light of what was happening in Poland.

Germany's invasion of France created a complicated political situation. In June 1940, Churchill offered France a fusion of states. Charles de Gaulle, the newly appointed French Under-Secretary for War, personally received the hastily drawn up offer and brought it to Paul Renaud,

---

Government Printing Office, 2012), 3-4.

[22]Ibid., 1.

[23]Mark Seaman, "A New Instrument of War: the Origins of the Special Operations Executive," in *Special Operations Executive: a New Instrument of War*, ed. Mark Seaman, *Studies in Intelligence Series* (New York, NY: Routledge, 2006), 8-11.

the French Prime Minister, who rejected it. Renaud resigned shortly thereafter and Marshal

Phillipe Pétain took his place. De Gaulle escaped the country, and Britain recognized him as the

leader of Free French people, but not the head of a government in exile. Pétain, however, sought

and achieved an armistice with Germany on 22 June.[24] The armistice resulted in two primary

territorial areas in France: one occupied by the Germans in the north and one governed by Pétain

in the south. Germany created a denied territory and very rapidly inspired resistance groups that

were willing to use force to overthrow the regime. Some of these groups were: *L'Armée Secréte*,

the *Maquis*, the *Francs Tireurs et Partisans*, and *Groupe de l'Armée*.[25]

Britain began its initial attempts to support these groups by employing the GS(R) and

Section D of the SIS.[26] In July 1940, Britain combined the organizations and designated them the

Special Operations Executive (SOE), thus establishing a transformed organization to conduct

UW.[27] Initial attempts to infiltrate France were rarely successful, the first occurring in August

1940 on boats borrowed from the Royal Navy.[28] The second successful attempt was by parachute,

Operation Savanna, which occurred in March 1941. Five Free French soldiers were parachuted

into France to sabotage a German U-boat facility; SOE extracted them with more boats acquired

from the Royal Navy when the sabotage mission failed. While the sabotage was a failure, they set

---

[24]M. R. D. Foot, *SOE in France: an Account of the Work of the British Special Operations Executive in France, 1940-1944* Foreign Intelligence Book Series (Frederick, M.D.: University Publications of America, 1984), 130.

[25]Forrest C. Pogue, *The Supreme Command*, United States Army in World War II: The European Theater of Operations (Washington, D.C.: Office of the Chief of Military History, Dept. of the Army, 1954), 152.

[26]Section D was MAJ Grand's organization within the larger SIS.

[27]Foot, *SOE in France*, 148; W. J. M. Mackenzie, *The Secret History of SOE: Special Operations Executive, 1940-1945* (London, UK: St Ermin's Press, 2000), 753-55.

[28]Sir Brooks Richards, "SOE and Sea Communications," in *Special Operations Executive: a New Instrument of War*, ed. Mark Seaman, *Studies in Intelligence Series* (New York, N.Y.: Routledge, 2006), 34; Foot, *SOE*, 92.

a precedent of integrating unconventional forces with conventional force units to insert and extract SOE agents in France, a practice that would continue for the duration of the war.[29] The SOE later inserted the first British operatives into France in May and the first supplies for resistance forces in June, both by parachute.[30] The successful execution of integrated operations encouraged British Chief of Air Staff Charles Portal to designate in August 1941 a specific air squadron (the 138th) for "special duties."[31] In fact, aerial delivery became the primary method of personnel and materiel distribution for the UW campaign in France.

The SOE also had an integrated organization that synchronized sustainment operations with UW operations. The mission operations (MO) section, later the Air Liaison (AL) section, coordinated with the U.K. Air Ministry to transport personnel and materiel into denied territory. The AL collected the SOE's transportation requirements from country-based sub-sections and provided them, with their associated priority, to the Air Ministry for allocation.[32] By designating a single movement coordinator, SOE simplified the process for consolidating and communicating requirements to the RAF, improving the efficiency of their sustainment operations.

The United States established an organization to perform similar missions in 1941: the office of the Coordinator for Information (COI). William J. Donovan spent the first two months of the year touring different British covert operations throughout Europe and the Middle East. With help from the British, Donovan convinced President Roosevelt to appoint him the COI on

---

[29]Foot, *SOE in France*, 154; Gordon A. Harrison, *Cross-Channel Attack*, United States Army in World War II: The European Theater of Operations (Washington, D.C.: Office of the Chief of Military History, Dept. of the Army, 1993), 201.

[30]Foot, *SOE in France*, 162-63, 65.

[31] Ibid., 165; M. R. D. Foot, *SOE: An Outline History of the Special Operations Executive, 1940-46*, Foreign Intelligence Book Series (Frederick, M.D.: University Publications of America, 1984), 95.

[32] Foot, *SOE in France*, 77.

July 11, 1941.[33] COI received sections from the Office of National Intelligence (ONI) and G-2 as well as the authority to use unvouchered funds from the President in November.[34] With these organizations and capabilities, COI developed a subordinate section with roles in guerrilla warfare parallel to those of the SOE. According to Kermit Roosevelt, Special Activities/Goodfellow (SA/G), led by MAJ M. Preston Goodfellow, had the stated purpose "to organize and execute morale and physical subversion, including sabotage, fifth column activities and guerrilla warfare."[35]

The COI grew to an office of 631 by March 1942.[36] COI established an internal board to establish priorities for materiel procurement. They also had a section designated to coordinate transportation for agents and materiel.[37] Both SO and the Special Intelligence Branch (SI) had internal supply sections. The communications branch had a special warehousing and shipping section designed specifically to provide communications materiel to the agents in the field.[38] Donovan met with Sir Colin Gubbins, the head of the SOE, in June. They agreed on splitting areas of effort across the globe within each organization would act. The SOE would focus initially on France, but the COI would assist once it had the personnel and materiel. They also agreed "there would be a complete interchange of intelligence, finance, equipment,

---

[33]Anthony Cave Brown, *The Last Hero: Wild Bill Donovan* (New York, NY: Times Books, 1982), 149-54; Foot, *SOE*, 173.

[34]Michael Warner, "The Office of Strategic Services: America's First Intelligence Agency," https://www.cia.gov/library/center-for-the-study-of-intelligence/csi-publications/books-and-monographs/oss/index.htm; Kermit Roosevelt, *War Report of the OSS (Office of Strategic Services)* (New York, NY: Walker Publishing Company, Inc., 1976), 85; Brown, *The Last Hero*, 176.

[35]Roosevelt, *War Report of the OSS*, 80.

[36]Brown, *The Last Hero*, 174.

[37]Roosevelt, *War Report of the OSS*, 83-89.

[38]Ibid., 140-41.

transportation, and plans in order to obtain economy of force."[39] This integration lasted throughout the UW campaign in France and ultimately resulted in robust and economical efforts to sustain the French resistance. It also allowed COI to focus their efforts on supporting the Allies in North Africa.

The SOE, however, continued their operations in France without assistance from the United States. SOE established two air liaison teams inside France in 1942: the *service d'atterrisages et parachutages* (SAP) to coordinate aerial resupply in the non occupied zone and the *bureau de opèrations aèriennes* (BOA) to do the same within the occupied zone. Both organizations coordinated materiel supply of the resistance fighters from Britain and North Africa.[40] SOE, at this point, had developed a fully integrated system of collecting supply and transportation requirements. They were able to prioritize, communicate and synchronize their requirements with conventional forces. The SAP and BOA provided the critical capabilities, in conjunction with De Gaulle's twelve military regional delegates (DRMs), to receive and issue materiel.[41] The SOE had developed a complete, integrated and effective distribution system between Britain and France two years before the Allied invasion of Normandy. This system, while numerically small, demonstrated the economical use of special operations personnel to perform sustainment functions normally performed by sustainment personnel.

The SOE increased the flexibility within their distribution network in 1943 through a system known as "depot grounds" to effectively deliver supplies. When aircrews were unable to locate a drop zone, or establish communication with agents designated to receive supplies, they would alter their flight path to pre-determined locations that anticipated receipt of supplies.[42]

---

[39]Brown, *The Last Hero*, 236-37.

[40]Foot, *SOE in France*, 226.

[41]Foot, *SOE*, 223.

[42]Foot, *SOE in France*, 86.

SOE agents established landing parties with resistance fighters that would operate nightly during periods of high lunar illumination. This flexible system provided materiel either directly to the team requesting it or the depot ground to build stocks. The RAF's ability to provide aerial support to the SOE was so effective, that the first OSS agents employed inside occupied France, Operation Penny Farthing, had to travel from North Africa to Britain in order to get into the country. There was no capability to transport them from North Africa to France. Penny Farthing remained in Southern France for the duration of the campaign, and ultimately provided intelligence and materiel to resistance fighters during Operation Dragoon.[43]

The OSS experienced two setbacks in 1943: communications supply and transportation allocation. Two former OSS agents, Stewart Alsop and Thomas Braden, wrote in 1946 that "an agent without a radio wasn't much of an agent, and the radio's value was far greater than its handicap."[44] In 1943, shipping space for the Strategic Services Transmitter-Receiver (SSTR-1) was unavailable or infrequent, resulting in a shortfall of the OSS' ability to provide agents the radio. To overcome the shortage Donovan ordered all individuals deploying to theaters accompanied with an SSTR-1. This simple system enabled the OSS to overcome the shortage and cease the practice. The other issue was the ability to obtain cargo space on deploying aircraft. Administrative requirements increased the amount of time required to prepare materiel for deployment. The OSS was able to secure blanket approval of tonnage from air providers in the Mediterranean theater in order to expedite the process.[45] The OSS frequently employed simple solutions to solve sustainment challenges.

---

[43]Brown, *The Last Hero*, 337, 561.

[44]Stewart Alsop and Thomas Braden, *Sub Rosa: The O.S.S. and American Espionage* (New York, NY: Reynal & Hitchcock, 1946), 46.

[45]Roosevelt, *War Report of the OSS*, 141.

The SOE experienced two major setbacks in 1943. First, the high success rate of parachute operations resulted in a shortage of parachute supplies. When SHAEF established the Maintenance by Air Committee in November, SOE built a stock of parachutes designed to sustain it through OVERLORD, seven months before the invasion of Europe.[46] Second, the Nazis compromised two important SOE networks from June until November 1943: Prosper and Scientist. The loss of agents and materiel increased sustainment requirements at a critical time leading up to the invasion. It took both the OSS and SOE to overcome these setbacks. They were both placed under SHAEF that fall and were designated Special Operations Executive/Special Operations (SOE/SO), later designated the Special Force Headquarters (SFHQ). The Mediterranean theater saw the establishment of a similar organization, the Special Project Operations Center (SPOC). SPOC adopted SOE's practice of consolidating requirements and communicating them to the conventional air force providers in the Mediterranean theater.[47] By May of 1944, both Northern and Southern France had integrated headquarters with control of the resistance movements.[48]

The US Air Force (USAAF) established the final critical operation for the UW campaign in December 1943, Operation Carpetbagger. The Air Force designated the 36th and 406th Bomb Squadrons, conventional air force units, to provide aerial support for SFHQ. Carpetbagger began operations on January 4/5, 1944 with six aircraft, and doubled in capability by January 22.[49] SFHQ was able to compensate for the lost materiel and personnel in France through additional

---

[46]Foot, *SOE in France*, 82.

[47]Harris G. Warren, *Special Operations: AAF Aid to European Resistance Movements 1943-1945* (Maxwell AFB, AL: Air Historical Office, 1947), http://www.afhra.af.mil/shared/media/document/AFD-090522-060.pdf. 42. This official AF historical file will be referred to as AAFRH-21 throughout.

[48]Pogue, *The Supreme Command*, 159, 300. SOE/SO was redesignated SFHQ in May, 1944 but will be referred to as SFHQ throughout.

[49]Warren, *AAFRH-21*: 60-61.

transportation support provided by conventional forces. The RAF also provided more air support to the resistance. On January 27, 1943, Churchill directed Portal to provide more aerial support to the resistance. The RAF came through providing in the first quarter of 1944 five times the quantity of supplies provided in last quarter of 1943.[50]

At the Churchill's direction, both OSS and SOE participated in an informal committee, beginning in January, 1944, that included the Air Ministry and De Gaulle's *Bureau central de Renseinements et d'Action* (Militaire) (BCRA). The organizations represented in this committee reflect what Marcel Vigneras states was its intended purpose: "to devise ways and means of increasing the flow of military equipment, because airlift rather than availability of materiel was still the limiting factor in supplying Resistance groups."[51] Integration of SFHQ with external organizations was so successful at sustaining the resistance forces that SHAEF approved the establishment of a staff to "co-ordinate all Allied activities in support" of the resistance forces. All resistance forces were designated the French Forces of the Interior (FFI) on June 6, and two weeks later the Etat-Major des Forces Francaises de l'Interieur (EMFFI) was established. The staff was composed of personnel from the OSS's SO directorate, the SOE's F and RF section, and the BCRA.[52]

SFHQ built up material and personnel in France in anticipation of both Operations Overlord and Dragoon. SFHQ initiated twenty-eight missions with SOE F section personnel between January 1 and June 1, 1944.[53] The USAAF began the Carpetbagger missions, which would lead to the large-scale daytime resupply of resistance fighters during the pursuit of the

---

[50]Foot, *SOE*, 222.

[51]Marcel Vigneras, *Rearming the French*, United States Army in World War II (Washington, D.C.: U.S. Army Center of Military History, 1957; repr., Reprint, 1982), 299-300. The BCRA was De Gaulle's organization in Britain designated to control the French resistance.

[52]Foot, *SOE in France*, xxii; Vigneras, *Rearming the French*, 300.

[53]Foot, *SOE in France*, 519.

Nazi retreat. SFHQ had prepared 276 American, British and French soldiers to be parachuted into France, referred to as "Jedburghs" after a town in Scotland.[54] The resistance forces surprised the Jedburghs often with their well-developed organization and freedom. They often had functioning hospitals, requisition, and supply systems.[55] Once a Jedburgh team collaborated with a resistance unit, aerial resupply to the guerrillas was soon to follow. The Jedburgh teams and OSS Operational Groups (OGs) made up the bulk of OSS participation in the UW campaign in France. The OGs were thirty man units divided into fifteen man teams composed of two officers, weapons and demolition experts, a communications expert and a medic.[56] In fact, the contemporary ODA's organizational design directly evolved from the OSS OG's design.

The success of the national uprising in conjunction with the Normandy landings is a topic of contention amongst historians. Harrison notes: "Not only was there no systematic recording of the facts of their operations, but there was no yardstick by which to measure the effectiveness of an irregular force, whose role was strategic, rather than tactical."[57] On the other hand, Foote tells us that "on the night of 'Neptune' [sic], D-1/D-Day, the French made 950 interruptions of their own railway system, considerably more (even if at less spectacular places) than the RAF and the USAAF had secured… over the previous two months."[58] Harrison points out what is probably the most relevant matter, that the role of the resistance, and therefore the SFHQ was strategic. The

---

[54]John Whiteclay Chambers, *OSS Training in the National Parks and Service Abroad in World War II* (Washington, D.C.: U.S. Dept. of the Interior, National Park Service, 2008), 323-24; Vigneras, *Rearming the French*, 304.

[55]Alsop and Braden, *Sub Rosa*, 132.

[56]John Whiteclay Chambers, "Office of Strategic Services Training in World War II," *Studies in Intelligence* 54, no. 2 (2010): 31-32.

[57]Harrison, *Cross-Channel Attack*, 207.

[58]Foot, *SOE*, 225. The disparity between their accounts can likely be attributed to either bias or the fact that Foote had a great deal of declassified information available to him in 1980 that Harrison did not have in 1950.

fact that the uprising occurred in conjunction with the Normandy landings is the mark of SFHQ's success. That success depended largely on coordination between SFHQ personnel and a multitude of conventional force units.

SPOC provided a unique capability in Dragoon that SFHQ did not in Neptune. Conventional air forces and some naval forces infiltrated both OGs and Jedburghs into southern France in the days leading up to the subsequent landing operations to Neptune. Operation Penny Farthing had been functional for over a year by the time of the Dragoon landings. It had developed into a 300-man network, providing intelligence directly to commanders during the moments they were waiting to land on the beaches of southern France.[59]

OSS and SOE operations in France from the time of the landings until the complete liberation of France is small in size and scope compared to the massive land armies that entered France in the summer of 1944. However, they had been fighting an unconventional war for four years by that point, and had one last contribution to make. An aerial resupply on July 14, 1944 set the example for successive daytime supply operations that provided the largest amount of materiel to the resistance yet seen.[60] From July to September of 1944, the RAF and USAF dropped 6,248 tons of materiel into France, more than the entire sum they had been able to in the previous three and a half years of war.[61] The OSS coordinated for almost fifteen percent of the total quantity of small arms ammunition provided to the French from the US during the entire war.[62] That may not seem to be a decisive contribution to the total war effort, but sustainment support to the resistance only had to be sufficient to keep the resistance active.

---

[59]Brown, *The Last Hero*, 581; Roosevelt, *War Report of the OSS*, 114.

[60]Brown, *The Last Hero*, 562-63; Foot, *SOE*, 227-28.

[61]Foot, *SOE in France*, 473.

[62]Vigneras, *Rearming the French*, 307, 402. The total quantity of small arms ammunition from provided by the OSS was 7,386,572 rounds and the United States contributed a total of 50,173,000 rounds.

The OSS and SOE provided the bulk of their materiel support to the French in a few daytime missions during a very short period of the war. It was, in fact, in conjunction with major combat operations across France after the Normandy landings. The 8th Air Force performed these missions to appease concerns of the U.S. Secretary of State that the U.S. contribution to the French resistance was equitable to the British contribution.[63] Three considerations are necessary before assessing these large-scale, daytime operations as successful. First, the airdrop on July 14, 1944 provided supplies to a resistance effort that was actually defeated and scattered by the Germans by July 21, 1944.[64] The historian Harris G. Warren provides the remaining two more important considerations in *AAFRH-21*. SOE and OSS objectives were to provide materiel to small groups over a large area. This was complete by the time of the land invasions. Finally, the aircraft were available at that time of the war only because their "diversion from strategic bombing was not serious."[65] The value of these specific airdrop operations are not, however, indicative of the entire success of the sustainment system established by the OSS and SOE. Evaluating this system in terms of economy, integration, and simplicity demonstrates its effectiveness.

The UW campaign was certainly economical for both the United States and Britain. The fact that the small arms support provided by the OSS to the resistance constituted only 15% of the overall U.S. contribution illustrates the small price the UW campaign cost compared to the total cost of the war. So do the facts that air support for guerrilla resupply was a lower strategic priority than the strategic bombing campaign and the ability of the air forces to quintuple their support over a three month period leading up to the invasion. Sustainment support to the French resistance fighters was clearly an economical way to put tactical pressure on the German Army.

---

[63]Ibid., 301, 04.

[64]Foot, *SOE*, 227-28.

[65]Warren, *AAFRH-21*: 74-75.

An outstanding capability that the SOE and OSS brought to the resistance were their ability to integrate support from a variety of sources. The SOE established procedures for utilizing both naval and air assets as early as 1941. They established integrated systems within their headquarters for collecting requirements and communicating them in both European and Mediterranean theaters. They also established organizations for the reception and distribution of materiel within France. This fully integrated system that included the ability to collect requirements, prioritize the, and effectively communicate them to external agencies capable of providing sustainment support enabled the resistance to culminate in a national uprising in conjunction with the Normandy landings.

Finally, the use of simple systems proved effective throughout the war. SOE and OSS were able to employ simple solutions to internal challenges, such as distributing equipment shortages to theater with deploying personnel. They also built simple systems to overcome challenges in France, such as establishing a single point of requirements collection for the entire theater. Both organizations actions demonstrate the utility of simple sustainment systems in UW.

SOE and OSS conducted UW campaigns throughout the globe during World War II. They operated in Northern Africa, Asia and the rest of Europe. In fact, the largest materiel operation they conducted was in support of Josip Broz Tito's partisan movement in Yugoslavia.[66] Ironically, British historian W. J. M. Mackenzie remarked that "bliss was it in that dawn to be alive" while referring to the timeframe in which Tito established a communist government there.[67] SOE and OSS simultaneously supported multiple Greek partisan movements. Both of these UW campaigns played a part in the next case study: Greece.

---

[66]Mackenzie, *The Secret History of SOE*, 440.

[67]Ibid., 433.

Greece

Historians have frequently divided the Greek Civil War into three rounds, or acts. The first round occurred between Greek resistance fighters during the German occupation between 1941 and 1944. SOE conducted a UW campaign during this timeframe that merits the attention of this study. The second round was mainly a civil war between Greek communists and multiple right-leaning resistance groups, who were supported by Britain. There was no UW campaign during the second round, but its events bear on the third round, in which there was. The seeds of the third round were planted long before it actually began in 1946, but the UW campaign began with the government of Greece declaring the communist movement within Greece illegal in 1947. Three of Greece's Balkan neighbors provided support to resistance organizations; however most available research material is related to Yugoslavia. Thus, the discussion about the third round that follows is mostly, but not singly, focused on the external support provided by Yugoslavia.

The First Round

In October 1940 Italy invaded Greece after having occupied Albania in 1939.[68] Greece, at the time a dictatorship under Ionnas Metaxis, successfully defended itself – but the nation soon lost its independence and national unity, and would not regain independence for nine years.[69] Germany rapidly occupied both Yugoslavia and Greece in April 1941, during the early stages of World War II.[70] The Germans entered Athens on April 27, 1941 and quickly established a quisling government.[71] By June 1 they secured Crete and established a viable line of

---

[68]Charles R. Shrader, *The Withered Vine: Logistics and the Communist Insurgency in Greece, 1945-1949* (Westport, CT: Praeger, 1999), xvii.

[69]C. M. Woodhouse, *Apple of Discord; A Survey of Recent Greek Politics in their International Setting* (London,UK: Hutchinson & Co., LTD, 1948), 9.

[70]Ibid., 21.

[71]During World War II the term 'quisling' referred to a person or organization that collaborated with the Nazis.

communication to North Africa.[72] The British Military Mission (BMM) departed quickly, and the

Greek government in exile abandoned Crete, establishing a presence in both Cairo and London.[73]

The conditions were ripe for a UW campaign against the quisling Greek government. SOE

maintained an office in Cairo, but lacked the clear organization and role that its higher

headquarters in the U.K. had. In a period of four years, SOE (Cairo) had four different names, and

eight different leaders (civilian and military) and these name and leadership changes had no clear

relationship to each other. C. M. Woodhouse, who served as a military advisor to Greek

resistance groups and later served in British Parliament, noted that SOE (Cairo) was so detached

from its agents in Greece that "four months after the first party of British parachutists had been

dropped in Greece, SOE Cairo could not even trace any record of their names."[74]

A brief outline of Greece's physical terrain is illustrates some of the differences between

the UW campaign in France and the two UW campaigns during the Greek Civil War. In 1945

Greece's total land area was approximately 50,000 square miles, a little larger than the states of

Pennsylvania and New Jersey combined.[75] Either coastal or mountainous regions made up most

of that terrain, and the two largest population centers were Athens and Salonika, both port cities.

The combined total of their population was less than 500,000 of the nation's entire population of

3.7 million.[76] Its international borders, which were established as the result of three different wars

---

[72]Hugh H. Gardner, *Guerrilla and Counterguerrilla Warfare in Greece (Draft), 1941-1945* (Washington, D.C.: U.S. Army Center of Military History, 1962), 18.

[73]Woodhouse, *Apple of Discord*, 42.

[74]Ibid., 45.

[75]Shrader, *The Withered Vine*, 2; Stephen Merrill, *The Communist Attack on Greece*, Special Report No. 15, 21st Regular Course, U.S. Strategic Intelligence School (Washington, D.C.: U.S. Strategic Intelligence School, 1952), 4.

[76]Evangelos Averoff-Tossizza, *By Fire and Axe: the Communist Party and the Civil War in Greece, 1944-1949*, 1st English language ed. (New Rochelle, N.Y.: Caratzas Brothers, 1978), 4; Statistical Office of the United Nations, *Demographic Yearbook 1948* (Lake Success, N.Y.: The United Nations, 1949), 82.

and followed no geographical or ethnic boundaries, were disputed with its neighbors Algeria, Yugoslavia, and Bulgaria.[77] Its transportation infrastructure was poorly developed with only roughly 10,000 miles of usable road and 2,000 miles of usable rail compared to Britain's 180,000 miles of road and 32,000 miles of rail.[78] The physical environment favored a guerrilla war because of a lack of infrastructure, harsh terrain and a large geographical area. A light guerrilla force would have a great deal of mobility compared to a mechanized conventional force.

The political situation in Greece was considerably complex. The country had a royal monarchy and an elected legislature with politicians from up to sixty different political parties.[79] This dearth of political parties naturally resulted in a corresponding dearth of resistance groups during the German occupation. Woodhouse, who advised Greek resistance movements throughout the war, wrote that the resistance organizations should not be viewed as homogenous groups where all members believed in the political positions of their leaders. He divided the Greeks, particularly those in the mountains, into "haves" and "have nots." This involved first drawing a horizontal line between the upper and lower economic groups, and then only drawing vertical lines separating political groups above the horizontal line, because this differentiation held little significance among those of low economic status. In *Apple of Discord*, while describing the separate groups, he wrote: "I come to the alphabetic designations which long constituted the whole of the English-speaking public's knowledge of the Greek resistance movement… I pause only to stress that for the last time that although the following designations formally penetrate below the horizontal line, it is only above it that they correspond to real differences."[80] In light of

---

[77]Shrader, *The Withered Vine*, 2.

[78]Edgar O'Ballance, *The Greek Civil War, 1944-1949* (New York, NY: Praeger, 1966), 22. O'Ballance notes that England (the country within Great Britain) and Greece are roughly the same size in terms of land area.

[79]Woodhouse, *Apple of Discord*, 12.

[80]Ibid., 56-59.

this view the SOE supported all resistance movements, even the communist, which became the largest Greek resistance movement by October 1944.[81]

According to Dominique Eudes, a French historian sympathetic to the Greek Communist Party (*Kommunistikon Komma Ellados or KKE*), the SOE's first agents dropped into Greece on 1 October 1942 were instructed to find the Greek National Democratic Union (*Ellinikos Dhimocraitikos Ethnikos Sindhesimos* or EDES).[82] EDES was a right-leaning resistance group that supported a republican government. Instead they first encountered the Greek People's Liberation Army (*Ellinikos Laikos Apeleftheretikos Stratos* or ELAS), which was the military arm of the KKE.[83] A third significant resistance organization is the National and Social Liberation (*Ethniki Kai Koinoniki Apeleftherosis* or EKKA), which was more liberal than EDES, but far from being communist.[84] Many more resistance movements were active in Greece at the time, but they lack significance within the scope this study. The SOE supported all three of these organizations in much the same way it did in France. It provided British military materiel (mainly small arms, ammunition and sometimes uniforms) and assisted with sabotage.[85]

Three actions by Greek resistance fighters merit particular attention. The first was the destruction of the Gorgopotomus Bridge and defeat of an Italian garrison on 25/26 November 1942. SOE intended the operation to occur in conjunction with operations in North Africa that had concluded three weeks earlier, so it did not achieve the overall objective the SOE desired. It remains significant, however, because the operation was supplied by the SOE, thus establishing

---

[81]Gardner, *Guerrilla and Counterguerrilla Warfare*, 45.

[82]Dominique Eudes, *The Kapetanios: Partisans and Civil War in Greece, 1943-1949*, trans. John Howe (New York, NY: Monthly Review Press, 1972), 15; Gardner, *Guerrilla and Counterguerrilla Warfare*, 12, 21.

[83]Gardner, *Guerrilla and Counterguerrilla Warfare*, 12, 18.

[84]Ibid., 22.

[85]Ibid., 38.

the precedents of integrated operations and using currency to motivate the guerrillas.[86] In June 1943, SOE coordinated Operation Animals, intended partly as a deception for Operation Husky, the Allied invasion of Sicily. Animals was largely successful, resulting in both the destruction of a militarily significant bridge and disruption of German lines of communication in forty-four separate locations during the month prior to execution of Husky. The success of Animals even led the Germans to redeploy a valuable Panzer division to the Peloponnese, reducing the available combat power to respond to the Allied forces in Sicily.[87] This was the last operation that SOE was able to gain ELAS's full cooperation. At this point in time, ELAS was reliant on SOE integration for materiel support. The third operation was a response to the Italian armistice on 3 September 1943. Both the Germans and ELAS disarmed and disbanded Italian military formations, but ELAS kept the materiel, reducing their reliance on SOE for materiel support. The SOE was able to retain the integrity of one Italian division, but ELAS divided the rest and detained most of the leadership for participating in a "Fascist plot."[88] This incident demonstrates the tenuous nature of UW operations, the significance of materiel support to their conduct, and the loyalties of involved parties. SOE lost much of its ability to influence ELAS from this point forward because ELAS established an independent source of supply. The greater materiel autonomy contributed to greater operational autonomy. ELAS actively chose to abandon its integration with SOE.

Just a month before the Italian Armistice, on 4 August 1943, the SOE completed construction of a 1,700 foot airstrip in Neraidha.[89] An SOE operative, Captain Denys Hamson, oversaw a group of local civilians in the operation of an active drop zone. SOE Cairo sent

---

[86]Foot, *SOE*, 235; Mackenzie, *The Secret History of SOE*, 452.

[87]Mackenzie, *The Secret History of SOE*, 459; Foot, *SOE*, 235.

[88]Mackenzie, *The Secret History of SOE*, 467.

[89]Gardner, *Guerrilla and Counterguerrilla Warfare*, 126.

supplies and funds to construct the drop zone. Hampton used these resources to employ his

reception party as a construction crew to build the strip.[90] This economical use of indigenous

persons to perform construction resulted in completion of a high quality airport available to the

SOE in occupied Greece. While the airstrip established a firm line of communication between

Cairo and northern Greece, it set conditions for a political clash between the KKE and the Greek

government-in-exile. The chief British Military Liaison Officer (BLO), Brigadier E. C. W.

Myers, flew with a party of KKE leadership to Cairo in order to hold political conferences with

the King of Greece and the British Foreign Office. Unsurprisingly, the conferences ended with

both the right and left even more firmly entrenched in their previous positions.[91] Woodhouse

described it as "a deadlock of mutual exhaustion."[92]

Shortly after Myers and the KKE representatives returned to Greece in September, open

fighting between ELAS and EDES broke out. This marked the end to any coordinated efforts

between the two guerrilla bands. Woodhouse attempted to stop the fighting by denying airdrops,

but this failed. He only denied aerial resupply to ELAS, actually escalating the tension between

the two guerrilla bands.[93] The Germans took advantage of the guerrilla's disorganized state of

affairs by simultaneously razing villages in the mountains and forcing the relocation and

dissolution of the previously combined headquarters of the resistance forces. They also

established "Security Battalions" composed of quisling Greeks, employing these units to

capitalize on the destabilizing security environment and set conditions for a German

withdrawal.[94] The conditions in Greece at the end of 1943 more closely resembled a civil war

---

[90]Ibid., 124.

[91]Mackenzie, *The Secret History of SOE*, 466-67.

[92]Woodhouse, *Apple of Discord*, 170.

[93]Gardner, *Guerrilla and Counterguerrilla Warfare*, 136-37.

[94]Ibid., 138; Mackenzie, *The Secret History of SOE*, 469.

between loosely organized groups with conflicting political ideologies than a UW campaign against an established government. SOE and the BMM continued to support the government in exile long after Germany withdrew.

The German withdrawal was complete by 4 November 1944. The British, realizing the imminent threat of ELAS, increased their military presence to 22,600 troops in Greece during November, with additional reserves and air capability in Italy.[95] However, nearly all of Greece was occupied by ELAS or under the political control of the KKE. Only Athens, a small part of Solinka and a few villages with BMM presence were outside communist control.[96] Fighting between ELAS and the British military broke out openly in December, but the Britain was able to force a truce by 11 January 1945.[97] On 12 February 1945 both members of the KKE and the "Hellenic Government" signed the Varkiza Agreement.[98] This document was effectively a cease-fire agreement that allowed for amnesty and demobilization of ELAS, a plebiscite to "decide on the Constitutional question," and elections for a democratic government.[99]

The conclusion that SOE contributed to the violence during the second round is incorrect. Both Mackenzie, in 1948, and a contemporary scholar, S. Stephen Shrader, found that seeds of civil were sewn long before the SOE and the BMM were in Greece.[100] The SOE supported ELAS for two years with materiel and military advice, but their political ideology was long in place before the BMM arrived. ELAS was well organized and equipped to attempt the overthrow of the

---

[95]Gardner, *Guerrilla and Counterguerrilla Warfare*, 196, 98.

[96]Woodhouse, *Apple of Discord*, 214.

[97]Ibid., 224.

[98]Ibid., 308-10. Woodhouse translates a portion of the Varkiza Agreement in Appendix I.

[99]Ibid., 310.

[100]Mackenzie, *The Secret History of SOE*, 483; S. Stephen Shrader, *British Military Mission to Greece (BMM), 1942-44* (Fort Leavenworth, KS: School of Advanced Military Studies, USACGSC, 2009), 42.

Greek government, but the majority of their equipment came from either captured Italian or German war materiel. SOE's economical support to the resistance movmeents prevented a proliferation of war materiel in ELAS' possession. The fact that ELAS cut ties with SOE after finding another source of materiel proves this. SOE's success lie in its economical provision of materiel and its integrated capabilities with conventional force units.

In the end, ELAS failed to seize power through military action. The UW campaign conducted by SOE and the BMM had supported all resistance movements, but the BMM and SOE took two effective measures to prevent ELAS from succeeding. First, the BMM ceased provision of arms, but not ammunition, in October 1943 when they realized the KKE's intent to establish a communist government upon the German withdrawal.[101] The second was ELAS's disarmament following the Varkiza agreement. Greece, however, remained unstable.

The Third Round

Eight different governments attempted to establish unity and stability within Greece between 1945 and 1946, but each one failed.[102] The KKE remained a legal political party until the end of 1947, when Greek-American cooperation resulted in a rapid series of events that culminated with the KKE declaring sovereignty. Woodhouse noted that in September 1947 the elected government was replaced by a "Liberal-Populist coalition…, the communist press was then suppressed in October; a joint Greco-American staff was formed to fight the guerrillas in November; [and] the right to strike was abolished in December…."[103] In response the KKE proclaimed the existence of the "First Provisional Democratic Government of Greece" over Radio

---

[101]Gardner, *Guerrilla and Counterguerrilla Warfare*, 164.

[102]Shrader, *The Withered Vine*, 45.

[103]Woodhouse, *Apple of Discord*, 279.

Free Greece on 24 December 1947.[104] From that point forward, any military aid provided to the

KKE by an outside source for the use of force to overthrow the Greek government qualifies as an

act of unconventional warfare based off of the definition provided in *JP 3-05*.[105] Yugoslavia,

Albania, and Bulgaria had been doing so for years, and they continued to do so for years after the

KKE became an illegal organization.

The Soviet Union assisted successful partisan movements in Yugoslavia and Bulgaria but

provided no direct assistance to the communist movement in Greece. During the first two rounds

the Soviet Union did nothing more than visit the KKE political apparatus and ELAS in the

summer of 1943. The exact details of the visit are unknown, but the KKE increased participation

with the national government within a month of the visit and continued to rely on the BMM for

support.[106] Despite the United States' perception that the Soviet Union directly supported the

KKE, the truth is that only its regional neighbors supported the KKE.[107] According to Markos

Vafiades, the military leader of the Greek Democratic army (GDA), the Soviet weapons that

ELAS surrendered were provided by Russian prisoners of war that made up the Security

Battalions.[108] The KKE even requested Soviet assistance through the Bulgarian Chairman of the

Council of Ministers, Georgi Dimitrov, but was told to wait.[109] Joseph Stalin, then the General

---

[104]Merrill, *The Communist Attack on Greece*, 32.

[105]*JP 3-05*, GL-13-14.

[106]Gardner, *Guerrilla and Counterguerrilla Warfare*, 180-81.

[107]John O. Iatrides, "Perceptions of Soviet Involvement in the Greek Civil War 1945-1949," in *Studies in the History of the Greek Civil War, 1945-1949*, ed. Lars Bærentzen, John O. Iatrides, and Ole Langwitz Smith (Copenhagen: Museum Tusculanum Press, 1987), 232. The U.S. Ambassador to Greece, Lincoln MacVeagh, believed the KKE was a 'fifth column' activity for the Soviet Union.

[108]Markos is quoted in Eudes, *The Kapetanios*, 286. The GDA was a distinctly different organization from ELAS formed in 1946.

[109]Iatrides, "Perceptions of Soviet Involvement in the Greek Civil War 1945-1949," 246.

Secretary of the Communist Part of the Soviet Union, is quoted as saying "that struggle has no prospects whatsoever" with respect to the KKE's attempt for revolution.[110] The revolutionary drive in Greece was certainly domestic, but its chances of success were marginal without external assistance.

Two influential men within the KKE served in political and military leadership positions particularly relevant to this study. The first, Nicholas Zachariadis, held the office of Secretary-General of the KKE when Germany invaded Greece. He was a Soviet-educated communist and had served as head of the KKE since 1931. He spent 1941-1945 in Dachau, detained by the Germans for obvious political reasons. He returned to Greece after the Allied liberation and quickly positioned himself again as the Secretary General. Having been absent for the previous four years of resistance, Zachariadis' perspective was still strongly influenced by his training in Moscow. His desire to gain support from the Soviet Union and subsequently with the Communist Information Bureau (Cominform) eventually contributed to the political division within the KKE that ultimately led to the KKE's failure to overthrow the Greek government in 1949.[111] He did, however, seek and acquire assistance from Greece's neighbors, both military and political. The second key individual, Markos Vafiades, commanded the GDA during the third round. The Central Committee of the KKE appointed Markos, a popular veteran of the first and second rounds of the war, to command of the GDA in August 1946. He worked with the BMM in Macedonia during the first round and served as the political advisor to the ELAS commander

---

[110]Fitzroy Maclean, *Disputed Barricade; the Life and Times of Josip Broz-Tito, Marshal of Jugoslavia* (London, U.K.: Jonathan Cape, 1957), 340.

[111]O'Ballance, *The Greek Civil War, 1944-1949*, 14, 30, 49, 115, 51. The Cominform was established by nine seperate countries in October 1947 in order to "cooordinate the activities of the Communist Parties and exchange information." Its initial members were the USSR, Yugoslavia, Poland, Romania, Hungary, Czechoslovakia and Bulgaria with members from communist parties in France and Italy; Averoff-Tossizza, *By Fire and Axe*, 242.

during the second round.[112] Throughout the third round he generally favored small-scale operations and favored a patient approach to achieving political power in Greece. In this view he stood in direct opposition to Zachariades, who favored establishment of a large, well organized military arm to achieve the KKE's political objectives.

The communist commune in Boulkes, Yugoslavia provides a useful example of external support to the KKE. The residents of Boulkes, an ethnically German town in Yugoslavia, joined in the German retreat of 1944, deserting the town.[113] Yugoslavia's government populated the commune with Greek displaced persons in 1945 as "an idyllic refuge from the bitterness of exile."[114] In other words, they made the town a safe haven for refugees – at least nominally. In truth, the Boulkes camp was more akin to a concentration camp. Eudes described it as "a place where good militants – not vicious, not clinically paranoid, not bloodthirsty, but hard-working, obedient, conscientious pragmatists, gentle but determined – found themselves practicing an elaborate system of mistrust in the name of revolution."[115] Instead of creating a commune that could cultivate its livelihood from the ground, its population was reliant on the Yugoslavian Army for subsistence.[116] Out of the total of roughly 3,000 occupants, it had in 1946 only 161 women and 30 children.[117] In truth, it was a complicated and resource intensive military training camp. Boulkes provided radio communication with Albania and Bulgaria, control of GDA forces

---

[112]Woodhouse, *Apple of Discord*, 62, 64, 208. The military arm of KKE during the first and second rounds was ELAS. There was no officially organized military arm after the Varkiza Agreement until Markos was appointed the commander of the GDA; O'Ballance, *The Greek Civil War, 1944-1949*, 122.

[113]Milan Ristovic, "The Bulkes Experiment: A "Greek Republic" in Yugoslavia 1945-1949," *Balkan Studies* 46(2012): 125.

[114]Eudes, *The Kapetanios*, 251.

[115]Ibid., 289.

[116]Ristovic, "The Bulkes Experiment," 127.

[117]Ibid., 131.

within its communications range, sustainment support of personnel within the camp and into Greece, political indoctrination, and propaganda materials production. The major differences between Boulkes and the rest of the locations where Yugoslavia provided aid to the GDA were it size and its location. It was far from the border, north of the Yugoslavian capital of Belgrade, where the rest were much closer to Greece. It was also, by far, the largest camp. In June 1947 it held 22,500 Greeks.[118] The GDA did not employ the methods instructed at Boulkes camp until later in the war.

Despite the support from its neighbors, the GDA still had a difficult time in 1946. It began the year short of its personnel recruitment goals, but still managed to increase guerrilla activity. Most significantly, the GDA's tactics reveal a good deal about its external sustainment support. First, the GDA began to move operations from populated to more rural areas because of the nascent United Nations (UN) presence.[119] This had the circumstantial benefit of facilitating local civilian sustainment support because the shift to rural bases shortened lines of communication and enhanced economy of support. The GDA also began to "tax" villages, taking payment in the form of livestock that provided a ready source of food – a practice adopted by ELAS earlier in the war.[120] This did not solve overall subsistence shortages, though, including the limited quantities of medical supplies provided by some of Greece's neighbors; this led the GDA to raid medical facilities and pharmacies inside Greece.[121] Finally, GDA fighters relied heavily on a cheap but effective method of attack: the road-side bomb. This tactic, typically employed because the guerrilla is not capable of direct engagement, had a great enough effect that civilian traffic would not even attempt to use the roads without the presence of a military convoy. Averoff

---

[118]Shrader, *The Withered Vine*, 178.

[119]Averoff-Tossizza, *By Fire and Axe*, 201.

[120]Ibid., 202; Shrader, *The Withered Vine*, 29.

[121]Averoff-Tossizza, *By Fire and Axe*, 269.

even claims that it was one of the GDA's "most effective weapons used."[122] Given these tactics employed by the GDA, Greece's neighbors provided limited, or economical external support. The GDA was forced to forage for subsistence, steal medical supplies, and modify its tactics because external support did not provide for all of its needs.[123] The GDA did, however, continue to fight for two more years.

As a matter of military policy, the KKE between 1945 and 1947 sought to avoid civil war. It adopted a specific concept of "self-defense." This loosely organized program centered on ten-man groups that could conduct self defense in three tiers: individual, mass strikes, and armed resistance by former ELAS members. The KKE designed this model to defend against a "fascist coup."[124] The organization external to the former ELAS members – the *aftoamyna* – operated in small three-man groups referred to as *yiafaka*. This simple system proved effective in providing intelligence, recruiting, and logistics support throughout the entire conflict.[125] The former ELAS members, led by Markos, remained in the mountains and continued small-scale guerrilla operations for almost all of 1947. Markos was able to grow the size of the GDA throughout the year. Between 1 March and 10 April 1947 the GDA conducted 91 raids, simultaneously "taxing" and recruiting villagers in support of the KKE's agenda. By the end of the spring the GDA numbered 18,000 and by August approximately 35,000.[126] This significant increase in size proportionately increased the logistical burden placed on their external support apparatus.

---

[122]Ibid., 203.

[123]Eudes, *The Kapetanios*, 284. Eudes claims less than 0.5% of the GDA's armament came from Greece's socialist neighbors, though he provides no source or evidence of this.

[124]Ole Langwitz Smith, "Self-Defence and Communist Policy," in *Studies in the History of the Greek Civil War, 1945-1949*, ed. Lars Bærentzen, John O. Iatrides, and Ole Langwitz Smith (Copenhagen: Museum Tusculanum Press, 1987), 162.

[125]Shrader, *The Withered Vine*, 61.

[126]Eudes, *The Kapetanios*, 292-93; Averoff-Tossizza, *By Fire and Axe*, 215.

Unfortunately for the GDA, though, the Greek government was beginning to establish control within the country. On 22 March 1947 the government declared martial law in response to right-leaning extremist groups in Athens.[127] This set conditions for legitimate military action against the GDA, which at the time was still organized primarily for self-defense. The Greek National Army's (GNA) first major aggressive action against the GDA – Operation Terminus – took place from 15 April to 26 May 1947. Terminus was successful for the government and resulted in considerable losses for the GDA. According to Averoff, the GDA lost "647 dead of which 100 were found frozen, about 100 wounded and 412 prisoners." The national army also captured livestock and seized dairy farms upon which the GDA relied upon for subsistence, thus targeting one of the GDA's key vulnerabilities.[128] The Greek government had finally seized the military initiative and achieved political ends through military means. With continued assistance from Western nations, Greece was on track to establish a secure and stable democratic nation.

Greece's neighbors were equally interested in supporting regional security, however three were governed by communist regimes. Yugoslavia, in particular, was a considerable source of support for the KKE and GDA, but a few relevant facts significantly influenced the nature and amount of support that it provided. For example, in 1947 the two nations shared a border approximately 200 kilometers long.[129] This provided a very broad area for the GDA to cross, and Yugoslavia left the border open for them to do so. The status of Macedonia, the area of land on both sides of the border, had long been a point of contention between the two nations, and it remained so at the time. There was even a specific ethnic resistance organization within the EAM that strove for Macedonian independence, the Macedonian National Liberation Front (*Naroden Osloboditelin Front*, or NOF). NOF followed KKE direction, but its primary goal was

---

[127]Eudes, *The Kapetanios*, 290-91; Averoff-Tossizza, *By Fire and Axe*, 218-19.

[128]Averoff-Tossizza, *By Fire and Axe*, 222.

[129]Merrill, *The Communist Attack on Greece*, 4.

Macedonian national independence.[130] Greece had similar border disputes with all three of its communist neighbors. However, the KKE and Greece's communist neighbors attempted to put aside their regional disputes and held a joint meeting at Bled, Yugoslavia in August 1947. All participants agreed to support the GDA militarily and establish a Joint Military Council, which the GDA would have to refer to "so that coordinated measures can be taken by the Council in the rear areas to meet the demands created by the operations."[131] Eudes asserts that this was an attempt by Tito to establish a Balkan federation, united under Yugoslavia.[132] The details remain a matter of debate; however, the dispute did serve to drive the wedge even further between Markos and Zachariades.

Markos resisted Yugoslav pressure to dominate the KKE, but Zachariades supported it. The organization achieved mixed results, but its existence illustrates the fact that Yugoslavia, which retained influence within the organization, militarily supported the GDA. Further, the GDA only conducted two military actions at the behest of the joint committee, neither of which were successful.[133] Zachariades finally dismissed the foreign representatives to the organization in 1949.[134] Nevertheless, through 1947 Tito continued to provide military training, materiel, medical support, and even entered into formal military agreements with the KKE. He maintained

---

[130] Andrew Rossos, "Incompatible Allies: Greek Communism and Macedonian Nationalism in the Civil War in Greece, 1943-1949," *The Journal of Modern History* 69, no. 1 (1997): 42.

[131] Shrader, *The Withered Vine*, 175; F. A. Voigt, *The Greek Sedition* (London, UK: Hollis & Carter, 1949), 252. Voit translates the agreement in Appendix I.

[132] Eudes, *The Kapetanios*, 297.

[133] Averoff-Tossizza, *By Fire and Axe*, 241.

[134] Shrader, *The Withered Vine*, 174-75; Averoff-Tossizza, *By Fire and Axe*, 234-35.

public sympathy for the KKE, but privately he informed at least one Western diplomat that his priority was developing Yugoslavia by achieving regional peace.[135]

Yugoslavia's support remained critical to the GDA, which in the fall of 1947 underwent some drastic military changes. The KKE held its Third Plenum from 12 to 15 September 1947. Only six of twenty-five "statutory members" of the central committee were present, and Zachariades took advantage of this. He pushed the committee to abandon the policy of 'self-defense' and guerrilla warfare. Instead, he favored establishing a larger conventional military structure.[136] On 24 December 1947 a "Free Democratic Greek Government" declared itself on Radio Free Greece, stating its first priority was "Mobilization of popular forces to liberate Greece."[137] This mobilization again increased the GDA's sustainment requirements, but the new political priority failed to mitigate any of the sustainment risks associated with a larger and more conventional military organization.

The beginning of transition from guerrilla tactics to conventional resulted almost immediately in a tactical failure. The GDA attempted its first conventional action against the village of Konitsa on 25 December 1947. Three months was not enough time to recruit enough additional troops or even to train the ones already in the GDA to conduct offensive operations against the GNA, which was rapidly developing in size and capability from U.S. support. GDA units that were authorized 1,400 men were likely to actually field 1,000 men.[138] Their first battle after abandoning guerrilla tactics was disastrous. They attempted to mass their artillery (a mere

---

[135]Elizabeth Barker, "Yugoslav Policy Towards Greece," in *Studies in the History of the Greek Civil War, 1945-1949*, ed. Lars Bærentzen, John O. Iatrides, and Ole Langwitz Smith (Copenhagen: Museum Tusculanum Press, 1987), 274.

[136]Eudes, *The Kapetanios*, 302. A "plenum" was a meeting of the KKE central committee. They were numbered sequentially after the election of a new central committee. Once a new committee was elected, the next plenum would again be the "First Plenum."

[137]O'Ballance, *The Greek Civil War, 1944-1949*, 158-59.

[138]Averoff-Tossizza, *By Fire and Axe*, 254.

"three 105mm guns, a few old 55-pounders, and every available mortar") and actually siege the village. The national army repelled them by 4 January and continued to pursue small skirmishes in the surrounding countryside until 15 January.[139] Meanwhile, in Athens, the government declared the KKE illegal and continued to develop its military strength with Western assistance. Eudes wrote that "the Democratic Army intoxicated itself with résumés of 1930s Russian strategy manuals, while the Americans happily went on colonizing Athens."[140] The GDA was developing a capability that was neither economical to its supporters nor well integrated.

The KKE in 1948 continued to suffer personnel casualties and tactical defeats at the hands of the Greek government. Two events demonstrate the seriousness of the dire situation that the party found itself in. The first was Operation Dawn, which the National Army conducted from 15 April to 26 May 1948. This operation resulted in GDA losses of both critical terrain in the mountainous region and a good deal of its man-power. Out of an estimated 5,800 total GDA members, one estimate of GNA losses was "610 dead guerrillas… plus 310 wounded and 995 self-defense personnel taken as prisoners."[141]

The GDA lost fully one-third of its manpower in that region in a span of forty-six days. The National Army continued throughout the year to attrite the GDA and push them closer to Greece's northern borders. Making matters worse, the communists began a campaign of abduction and exportation of Greek children to foreign countries, compounding the GDA's need for external support. Averoff reasons that "the KKE wished to have… a considerable number of young militants, fanatic and well indoctrinated."[142] Voigt describes the nature of that indoctrination – the communists sought to "indoctrinate and train them for subversion, sedition,

---

[139]Eudes, *The Kapetanios*, 308.

[140]Ibid., 313.

[141]Averoff-Tossizza, *By Fire and Axe*, 251.

[142]Eudes, *The Kapetanios*, 262.

conspiracy against their fellow Greeks and to become the docile instruments of a future Communist tyranny."[143] The KKE claimed the abductions were to protect the children from the government's military operations, but the claim fails to address the fact that tactical units were drastically undermanned.[144] Until then, children and women had typically provided sustainment support only as non-combatants, but by 1949 the GDA had resorted to forced recruiting and the use of women and children in combat roles.[145]

On 28 June 1948 the Cominform very publicly denounced Yugoslavia and Tito. Yugoslavia continued to aid to the Greek rebels, and the GDA happily accepted the aid, but neither attempted to address the political issue of allegiance to Tito and Yugoslavia or Stalin and the Soviet Union. The United States considered Yugoslavia's support to the GDA as "de facto recognition" of the Free Democratic Greek Government, so the United States, as well as Britain, exerted diplomatic pressure on Yugoslavia to cease support to the GDA. The diplomatic efforts did not achieve instantaneous results, but eventually both the United States and Britain established trade agreements with Yugoslavia, giving them leverage to coerce Yugoslavia to cease its support to the GDA. As a result, the UN Special Committee on the Balkans noted a decrease in materiel support from Yugoslavia by September.[146] Yugoslavia's support to the GDA continued to decline until Tito officially closed the border a year later, effectively bringing it to an end.

---

[143]Voigt, *The Greek Sedition*, 195.

[144]Averoff-Tossizza, *By Fire and Axe*, 260-61.

[145]O'Ballance, *The Greek Civil War, 1944-1949*, 168, 92. O'Ballance notes that in 1948 the UN Balkan Commission was informed by the Red Cross that 23,696 children had been detained by the communists; Averoff-Tossizza, *By Fire and Axe*, 261. Averoff recorded that 28,000 children had been abducted by 1949.

[146]Barker, "Yugoslav Policy Towards Greece," 275, 82, 86-87.

The remainder of 1948 went largely in the GDA's favor. It continued the tactic of seizing small villages and holding them for a time in order to "recruit" and "tax." One battle in the Vitsi mountain region, which butted up against the Albanian border, ended on 14 September 1948 with two battalions of the National Army refusing to fight.[147] While the GDA experienced a resurgence during the second half of 1948, especially in the central and southern parts of the country, this did not last – largely because of Greek disruption of the GDA's external support. One tactical event in particular sheds light on the nature of Albanian support to the GDA. In September 1948 a fishing boat provoked the attention of a Greek National Navy vessel, which gave pursuit. The GDA and the fishing boat attempted an ambush of the naval vessel, but to no avail. Upon its capture, the vessel was found to have had an Albanian captain and Greek guerrilla crew. Its contents included "2,000 German rifles, 100 machine-guns, 3,000 mines, and [sic] large quantities of ammunition, hand grenades, and KKE propaganda material."[148] The Albanians had established a naval distribution network to the Peloponnese because they did not have a land-based line of communication. This is evidence of a well-integrated sustainment infrastructure because of the correlation between its establishment and the increase in GDA operations in the Peloponnese. The Greek navy's interdiction of this flexible line of communication enabled the isolation of the GDA in the Peloponnese; by March of the following year Greece claimed that it had cleared the Peloponnese of GDA forces.

The KKE held its fifth plenum in January 1949. Two outcomes of this session directly contributed to the final defeat of the GDA that year. The first was Markos' relief as the commander of the GDA and the dismissal of Yugoslavia's military advisors to the GDA.[149] From

---

[147]Averoff-Tossizza, *By Fire and Axe*, 295. The remainder of the largest battles during the war occurred in the same region, as Albania became the primary source of external support to the GDA and the government began to eliminate the GDA throughout the rest of the country.

[148]Ibid., 299-300.

[149]Ibid., 319; O'Ballance, *The Greek Civil War, 1944-1949*, 185.

this point forward the GDA almost completely abandoned guerrilla warfare and employed conventional tactics. It established two large bases in the Grammos and Vitsi which ultimately served as easy targets for the Greek National Army. The second was the KKE's change in position regarding the issue of Macedonia. Up to that point the KKE desired a unified Greece with Macedonia as one of its partitions. At the fifth plenum the KKE announced its support of a free and independent Macedonia.[150] This aligned the KKE's policies with Bulgaria, which alienated both Yugoslavia and the NOF, the political body of the GDA's Macedonian contingent. In short, the KKE alienated its Yugoslav supporters and adopted the precise tactical methods that the Greek National Army was best prepared to counter. This precluded the GDA's ability to integrate with Yugoslavia and left it reliant on Albania, a power that was far less capable of providing the assistance the movement previously enjoyed.

The rest of 1949 was a series of GDA defeats. In March the government was able to claim the clearance of the Peloponnese. A victory in Roumeli, in June, ended the resistance in central Greece. Tito officially closed the border between Greece and Yugoslavia in July. Finally, the national army cleared both the Grammos and Vitsi regions of the GDA in August.[151] External support was clearly necessary for the GDA throughout the conflict. The fact that the GDA's defeat followed shortly after the conclusion of Yugoslavia's support demonstrates the reliance of resistance movements on external support. Evaluating that support in terms of economy, integration and simplicity reveal a good deal about the Greek Civil War.

Yugoslavia's support was economical for Yugoslavia. The country was devastated at the conclusion of World War II: it lost over 10% of its population; vast amounts of infrastructure was destroyed; and the transportation capability within the country was reduced by nearly half. By 1946 the communist country was beginning to receive war reparations in response to claims in

---

[150] Averoff-Tossizza, *By Fire and Axe*, 323.

[151] O'Ballance, *The Greek Civil War, 1944-1949*, 189, 94-99.

41

the billions of dollars.[152] It was not in a position to provide any great deal of support to the KKE. Except for the camp at Boulkes, the support consisted mostly of physical refuge and limited materiel support. The fact that the GDA relied on captured enemy materiel illustrates just how limited Yugoslavian aid was at this point in the conflict. It could not provide everything that the GDA needed. When the GDA attempted to transform into a large conventional force, not only was Yugoslavia no longer willing to support it, but Albania was incapable of doing so. Further, when Yugoslavia ceased its support to the GDA, it suffered no loss. In fact, because it ended up with trade agreements with both the United States and Britain, the country was better off than when it did support the GDA.

The support provided to the GDA was also well integrated until the fifth plenum. The meeting at Bled in 1947 resulted in two examples of integrated support to the GDA. The first is the assignment of Yugoslavian advisors to the GDA headquarters for two years. Even though Zachariades disliked the integrated headquarters, the GDA continued to fight for two years with Yugoslavian representation. After the fifth plenum, when Zachariades replaced Markos with himself and dismissed the Yugoslav advisor, the GDA lasted for only eight months. The second example of effective integration is the guerrilla reliance on Albanian sea based sustainment in the Peloponnese during 1948, which was also a stipulation of the agreement at Bled. The GDA was able to maintain a nation-wide resistance movement because its supporters could integrate more than one mode of sustainment support. While the abandonment of guerrilla tactics is commonly considered the reason for the GDA's defeat, it should also be noted that the organization had lost its ability to integrate with its external support.[153]

---

[152]Jozo Tomasevich, "Postwar Foreign Economic Relations," in *Yugoslavia*, ed. Robert J. Kerner, *The United Nations Series* (Berkeley and Los Angeles, CA: University of California Press, 1949), 390-92, 421-22. Tomasevich narrates particularly dismal economic conditions in much greater detail. Yugoslavia submitted claims of $1.3 and $11 Billion against Italy and Germany, respectively.

[153]Andrew R. Molnar, *Undergrounds in Insurgent, Revolutionary, and Resistance*

Finally, simple sustainment systems proved to be the most effective for the GDA. The GDA relied on the yiafaka for the duration of the entire conflict. These small, secretive three-man cells reliably provided intelligence, recruiting, and sustainment support. When the GDA transitioned to its most advanced organizational structure in 1949, it still relied on the yiafaka for support. The transition to a larger, more complicated organizational structure did not provide the resistance movement with a better sustainment capability than it already had.[154]

CONCLUSIONS AND RECOMMENDATIONS

The three UW campaigns above reveal a great deal about the nature of UW sustainment. Specifically, they demonstrate the need for economical, integrated, and simple sustainment of units conducting UW. These enduring aspects of the nature of UW sustainment should influence the design of the U.S. Army's GSB because the GSB is an enduring organization within the U.S. Army's conduct of UW. A design based off the last ten years of U.S. military experience in Iraq and Afghanistan, like the one proposed by the Band V FDU, does not properly address these aspects of UW. The GSB must be capable of providing economical, integrated, and simple sustainment support to the SFG in UW.

UW is an economical approach to war because it uses an external military apparatus to accomplish military objectives. The GSB's force structure should take into account the economical requirements of UW. Specifically, the unit does not require a larger quantity of common user land transportation (CULT) than it already has.[155] The CULT assets assigned to the

---

Warfare (Washington, D.C.: American University, 1963), 296; David Galula, *Counterinsurgency Warfare: Theory and Practice* (St. Petersburg, FL: Hailer Publishing, 1964), 12. Both scholars attribute the GDA's defeat to the abandonment of its guerrilla methods.

[154]Shrader, *The Withered Vine*, 100. In 1949 the GDA actually had three logistics battalions.

[155]CULT assets include cargo trucks, maintenance recovery vehicles, and refrigeration vans.

43

GSB would not doctrinally enter the UWOA. The case studies above demonstrate that the most effective distribution systems within the UWOA are those based on air, sea, or indigenous transportation platforms. This indicates that the GSB, which supports the UW campaign from a geographically separated location, does not need to conduct land distribution of sustainment support within the UWOA. Instead, it must conduct distribution outside the UWOA and coordinate for distribution assets to points within the UWOA.

The critical capability that the GSB provides to the SFG is its ability to integrate with external support providers. As the case studies above have shown, the sustainment organization within the UWOA must integrate with diverse external support providers. This extends beyond transportation capabilities, such as air and watercraft. They must also be able to coordinate for specific and appropriate supply and maintenance support. The support operations (SPO) section of the GSB should be designed to manage and coordinate all sustainment operations within the SFG.

Finally, the sustainment architecture in a UW campaign must be simple. All three case studies demonstrate that a sustainment system within UW benefits from simplicity. The GSB's supported units need a simple sustainment network that is capable of supporting all of their sustainment requirements. The GSB should be capable of coordinating sustainment support from all levels of sustainment organizations. Not only do SFG subordinate units already coordinate for other support from all levels of support organizations, but the GSB capability to coordinate for operational and strategic level sustainment support would reduce the complications resident in a robust sustainment architecture.

The design of the conventional BCT sustainment architecture is an appropriate structure for conventional forces employed in conventional warfare. UW, however, is the primary mission of SF, so its organizational design must be optimized for UW. Basing the design off of the conventional force structure or "dwell to deployment ratios" does not address the unique

44

requirements of UW.[156] The operational environment is such that the capabilities that SF provides will continue to be of value to the United States. SF is likely to continue operational employment in theaters with far less sustainment infrastructure than the ones in Iraq and Afghanistan (which themselves did not possess robust infrastructure until the U.S. government invested many years, dollars, and contractors to create it). SF's mission, based off its capability to conduct UW, is scalable from small three-man teams to an entire SFG serving as a CJSOTF. The Army must design the GSB in an economical, integrated, and simple manner in order to maximize its ability to sustain SF's core mission of unconventional warfare.

---

[156]These ratios are calculated by an individual Soldiers' time spent at his assigned duty station (dwell) to his time spent deployed (deployment).

BIBLIOGRAPHY

Alsop, Stewart, and Thomas Braden. *Sub Rosa: The O.S.S. And American Espionage.* New York, NY: Reynal & Hitchcock, 1946.

Averoff-Tossizza, Evangelos. *By Fire and Axe: The Communist Party and the Civil War in Greece, 1944-1949.* 1st English language ed. New Rochelle, N.Y.: Caratzas Brothers, 1978.

Barker, Elizabeth. "Yugoslav Policy Towards Greece." In *Studies in the History of the Greek Civil War, 1945-1949*, edited by Lars Bærentzen, John O. Iatrides and Ole Langwitz Smith. Copenhagen: Museum Tusculanum Press, 1987.

Brown, Anthony Cave. *The Last Hero: Wild Bill Donovan.* New York, NY: Times Books, 1982.

Chambers, John Whiteclay. "Office of Strategic Services Training in World War II." *Studies in Intelligence* 54, no. 2 (June 2010): 23-48.

———. *OSS Training in the National Parks and Service Abroad in World War II.* Washington, D.C.: U.S. Dept. of the Interior, National Park Service, 2008.

Department of Defense. *Joint Publication 3-05, Special Operations.* Washington, D.C.: Government Printing Office, 2011.

Eudes, Dominique. *The Kapetanios: Partisans and Civil War in Greece, 1943-1949.* Translated by John Howe. New York, NY: Monthly Review Press, 1972.

Foot, M. R. D. *SOE in France: An Account of the Work of the British Special Operations Executive in France, 1940-1944.* Foreign Intelligence Book Series. Frederick, M.D.: University Publications of America, 1984.

———. *SOE: An Outline History of the Special Operations Executive, 1940-46.* Foreign Intelligence Book Series. Frederick, MD: University Publications of America, 1984.

Gaddis, John Lewis. *The Landscape of History: How Historians Map the Past.* Oxford, N.Y.: Oxford University Press, 2002.

Galula, David. *Counterinsurgency Warfare: Theory and Practice.* St. Petersburg, FL: Hailer Publishing, 1964.

Gardner, Hugh H. *Guerrilla and Counterguerrilla Warfare in Greece (Draft), 1941-1945.* Washington, D.C.: U.S. Army Center of Military History, 1962.

Harrison, Gordon A. *Cross-Channel Attack.* United States Army in World War II: The European Theater of Operations. Washington, D.C.: Office of the Chief of Military History, Dept. of the Army, 1993.

Iatrides, John O. "Perceptions of Soviet Involvement in the Greek Civil War 1945-1949." In *Studies in the History of the Greek Civil War, 1945-1949*, edited by Lars Bærentzen, John O. Iatrides and Ole Langwitz Smith. 324 p. Copenhagen: Museum Tusculanum Press, 1987.

Mackenzie, W. J. M. *The Secret History of SOE: Special Operations Executive, 1940-1945.* London, UK: St Ermin's Press, 2000.

Maclean, Fitzroy. *Disputed Barricade; the Life and Times of Josip Broz-Tito, Marshal of Jugoslavia.* London, U.K.: Jonathan Cape, 1957.

McRaven, William H. "Posture Statement of Admiral William H. McRaven, USN, Commander,

United States Special Operations Command." (March 6, 2012).

Merrill, Stephen. *The Communist Attack on Greece*. Special Report No. 15, 21st Regular Course, U.S. Strategic Intelligence School. Washington, D.C.: U.S. Strategic Intelligence School, 1952.

Molnar, Andrew R. *Undergrounds in Insurgent, Revolutionary, and Resistance Warfare*. Washington, D.C.: American University, 1963.

O'Ballance, Edgar. *The Greek Civil War, 1944-1949*. New York, NY: Praeger, 1966.

Pogue, Forrest C. *The Supreme Command*. United States Army in World War II: The European Theater of Operations. Washington, D.C.: Office of the Chief of Military History, Dept. of the Army, 1954.

Richards, Sir Brooks. "SOE and Sea Communications." In *Special Operations Executive: A New Instrument of War*, edited by Mark Seaman. Studies in Intelligence Series, xv, 239 p. New York, N.Y.: Routledge, 2006.

Ristovic, Milan. "The Bulkes Experiment: A "Greek Republic" in Yugoslavia 1945-1949." *Balkan Studies* 46 (2007 2012).

Roosevelt, Kermit. *War Report of the OSS (Office of Strategic Services)*. New York, NY: Walker Publishing Company, Inc., 1976.

Rossos, Andrew. "Incompatible Allies: Greek Communism and Macedonian Nationalism in the Civil War in Greece, 1943-1949." *The Journal of Modern History* 69, no. 1 (1997): 42-76.

Seaman, Mark. "A New Instrument of War: The Origins of the Special Operations Executive." In *Special Operations Executive: A New Instrument of War*, edited by Mark Seaman. Studies in Intelligence Series. New York, NY: Routledge, 2006.

Shrader, Charles R. *The Withered Vine: Logistics and the Communist Insurgency in Greece, 1945-1949*. Westport, CT: Praeger, 1999.

Shrader, S. Stephen. *British Military Mission to Greece (BMM), 1942-44*. Fort Leavenworth, KS: School of Advanced Military Studies, USACGSC, 2009.

Smith, Ole Langwitz. "Self-Defence and Communist Policy." In *Studies in the History of the Greek Civil War, 1945-1949*, edited by Lars Bærentzen, John O. Iatrides and Ole Langwitz Smith. Copenhagen: Museum Tusculanum Press, 1987.

Statistical Office of the United Nations. *Demographic Yearbook 1948*. Lake Success, N.Y.: The United Nations, 1949.

Tomasevich, Jozo. "Postwar Foreign Economic Relations." In *Yugoslavia*, edited by Robert J. Kerner. The United Nations Series. Berkeley and Los Angeles, CA: University of California Press, 1949.

U.S. Army. Army Doctrine Publication 4-0, *Sustainment*. Washington, D.C.: Government Printing Office, 2012.

———. Field Manual 3-05.140, *Army Special Operations Forces Logistics*. Washington, D.C.: Government Printing Office, 2009.

———. Field Manual 3-18, *Special Forces Operations*. Washington, D.C.: Government Printing Office, 2012.

————. Training Circular 18-01, *Special Forces Unconventional Warfare*. Washington, D.C.: Government Printing Office, 2011.

United States Army Special Forces Command (Airborne). "Operational and Organization Concept Paper for USASFC(A) Changes to the SF Group(A)." 2009.

————. "Organization Design Paper for USASFC(A) Changes to the Special Forces Group(A)." 2009.

United States Joint Forces Command. "The Joint Operating Environment 2010." 2010.

United States Special Operations Command. "USSOCOM History." http://www.fas.org/irp/agency/dod/socom/index.html.

Vigneras, Marcel. *Rearming the French*. United States Army in World War II. Edited by Kent Roberts Greenfield Washington, D.C.: U.S. Army Center of Military History, 1957. Reprint, 1982.

Voigt, F. A. *The Greek Sedition*. London, UK: Hollis & Carter, 1949.

Warner, Michael. "The Office of Strategic Services: America's First Intelligence Agency." https://http://www.cia.gov/library/center-for-the-study-of-intelligence/csi-publications/books-and-monographs/oss/index.htm.

Warren, Harris G. *Special Operations: AAF Aid to European Resistance Movements 1943-1945*. Maxwell AFB, AL: Air Historical Office, 1947. http://www.afhra.af.mil/shared/media/document/AFD-090522-060.pdf.

Woodhouse, C. M. *Apple of Discord; a Survey of Recent Greek Politics in Their International Setting*. London,UK: Hutchinson & Co., LTD, 1948.